W9-AOU-037

Ironkid

Story by Dianne Wolfer

Illustrations by Margaret Krajnc

PM Plus Chapter Books
Ruby

U.S. Edition © 2013 Houghton Mifflin Harcourt Publishing Company
125 High Street
Boston, MA 02110
www.hmhco.com

Text © 2003 Cengage Learning Australia Pty Limited
Illustrations © 2003 Cengage Learning Australia Pty Limited
Originally published in Australia by Cengage Learning Australia

All rights reserved. No part of this work may be reproduced or transmitted in any form or by
any means, electronic or mechanical, including photocopying or recording, or by any information
storage and retrieval system, without the prior written permission of the copyright owner unless
such copying is expressly permitted by federal copyright law. Requests for permission to make
copies of any part of the work should be addressed to Houghton Mifflin Harcourt Publishing
Company, Attn: Contracts, Copyrights, and Licensing, 9400 Southpark Center Loop, Orlando,
Florida 32819.

10 11   1957   18
26517

Text: Dianne Wolfer
Illustrations: Margaret Krajnc
Printed in China by 1010 Printing International Ltd

Ironkid
ISBN 978 0 75 786897 9

Contents

Chapter One

Surf Club

I love floating on top of the ocean, watching fish and other creatures swim by. But once a week during the summer, something else happens.

I'm a junior member of the surf club and every Saturday morning we learn things. How to spot rips or strong currents in the sea. What to do if you get into trouble. Basic first-aid and other things like that.

My dad was surf club champion when he was young and now he's president. Dad sometimes lets me help on patrol. Being a lifeguard is fun.

The only thing I don't like about surf club are the races. Our coach is patient and most of the kids are good sports. I know that racing makes us push ourselves to become faster, but I prefer taking it easy at the beach.

I love swimming slowly over rocks looking for sea urchins. I think I'd like to be a marine biologist when I grow up. I already know the names of many different anemones and jellyfish.

Other days I think I might be an artist, because I really like to paint and draw. But I'm really into writing, too. Maybe I'll be a writer!

Dad calls me "the scientist" or sometimes "the painter." They're cool nicknames, but I also have another nickname. One that I really hate; it's "Zack, the dreamer."

People are always calling me that. Especially my teachers! What they don't realize is that I'm not dreaming, I'm thinking! Thinking about the beach and discovering new sea creatures. Thinking about painting, writing – all sorts of things!

When people say, "Zack's dreaming again," I'm actually planning!

I tried to explain this to my teacher once, but she just raised her eyebrows.

"You certainly have a good imagination, Zack."

"It's true," I protested.

"Maybe, but you still have to finish your math during recess."

Chapter Two

The Challenge

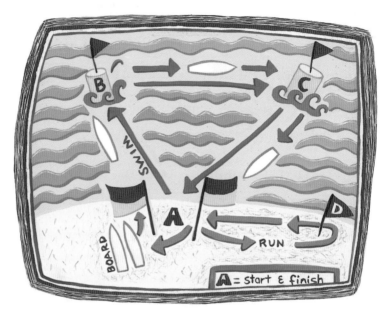

The summer is nearly over when it's time for the surf club Ironkid competition. The race is like an Ironman or Ironwoman contest, only for kids.

You begin with a run on the beach, then a long swim, next a board race, and finally, if your legs will carry you, another short run on the beach. It's a killer!

My swimming has never been very strong, and to stop Mom's worrying, last winter I took some lessons. "If you're going to spend your life in the water," she said, "you need to become a stronger swimmer. The ocean is so unpredictable …"

The lessons helped and my freestyle really improved. So now that I'm in a higher level, I can enter the Ironkid race. The question is, do I want to? I guess this is typical of me – everyone wishes I would dream less and *do* more.

Dad always competes in the Ironman and every year he comes in about fifth. I've never been interested in racing before, but this summer, for some weird reason, I feel like entering. Part of me really wants to give it a try. I think it would make my dad pretty proud, too.

Chapter Three

The Swim

It's too late to back out now. The race is about to begin and family and friends are here to watch.

It doesn't bother me that I'll probably come in last. I just don't want to come in last by a long way. But even *that* would be better than not making the distance!

The other kids look fit. Carl and Nathan are warming up and stretching their toned muscles. I glance down at my stick-insect body and sigh.

Our coach, Bill, calls us over. "Now, I'm going to say it again. You don't *have* to do this race. It's twice the distance you usually go. The conditions are rough today, and there's a rip over by the rocks. It could be tough going, so I want everyone to check again with a parent that you're *allowed* to go out."

I stare at the buoy floating way out in the bay, then look at Dad. He raises one eyebrow. I know he won't think less of me if I pull out, but I'm tired of everyone thinking I'm just a dreamer. I look back at the buoy and know I have to try.

"OK," Bill says. "This is similar to the adults' race. First, you run around the flag." He points down the beach. "Then you swim around the two buoys, come back in, grab a board, paddle around the buoys, come in, and run along the beach to the flag. Any questions?"

We look at each other and shake our heads.

"OK? It's run, swim, paddle, run. Is everyone ready?"

We nod.

"On your marks, get set, go!"

We run down the beach toward the flag. Carl and Nathan are in front. Of course! They splash through the surf as I'm rounding the flag.

I pull on my goggles, jump over the first wave, and feel my body tingle. The cold seawater always gives me a shock. I flick my legs the way Dad's shown me, dive under a cresting wave, and begin kicking. The ocean feels good.

A school of silvery fish dart away, and on the sand below, I can see a crab crawling toward a rock. How would the sea look from a crab's eye, I wonder. I bet I could write a good haiku poem about that.

I turn my head to breathe. There's no-one beside me. I look around. They're all way ahead. Oh no! I'm the last!

"Focus!" I tell myself. "This is a race – concentrate!" I turn to line up with the buoy and feel the frightening pull of a rip. I kick harder and my arms bite into the waves. No progress.

"Don't panic," I whisper. "You've been in rips before. Don't fight, swim across it."

I calm my breathing as I angle my body to escape.

Two lifeguards are nearby, in the rubber raft, watching me. It would be so easy to raise one arm and let them come and get me. Then I remember how pleased Dad looked when I decided to give the race a go.

My swimming feels strong. I can handle this rip. I point my body toward the buoy again, kick, and feel my body glide free.

As I turn my head to breathe, I do a quick calculation. About fifteen yards to the first buoy.

I drag my cupped hands through the water and catch up to my friend Dave, the nearest swimmer. We pace each other until I pull away at the second buoy. Yahoo, I'm not last anymore!

Carl and Nathan are way ahead, but that's okay. They're always way ahead! I pass someone else. Jim maybe. Now I'm right behind the main pack.

We're swimming back to shore. I catch a few waves and bodysurf toward the clubhouse.

As I run up the beach, I recognize Dad's voice in the crowd.

"Good for you, Zack!"

My legs run faster. I'm not last!

Chapter Four

The Paddle

Despite Dad's encouragement, I've never felt comfortable on a board. I love the feel of the water too much. I want to dive into the waves, not float on top of them like a bath toy.

Dad runs alongside me. "That was a great swim. I saw you battling the rip. Two of the others have pulled out. If you want to stop now, it would still be a mighty effort." Dad is offering me an honorable exit. It's tempting.

I look out to sea. Nathan and Carl are at the first buoy. They're still neck and neck, with five or six others trailing along behind.

I smile and grab a board. I don't know why I want to keep going. I'm not usually competitive. I just know that today I have to finish.

"Thanks, Dad, but I want to keep going."

He slaps my back and sprints through the first wave with me. "Okay, just watch that rip. If you get into trouble, raise your hand and we'll be out to help!"

"Okay."

I jump onto my board and feel the waves knock me around. I fight back and look for the first buoy. It keeps disappearing behind the swell. "You can do it," I mutter. "Focus!"

I pass the breakers and kick as hard as I can. The main pack is stretching out. I look up. Jim smiles in sympathy as he passes me. He knows I hate board racing. Only Dave is behind me now, and he's gaining. I kick harder. Stupid board. I wish I could fling it away and swim.

As I paddle, I wonder why I don't take after Dad more. He's a natural on a board. Everyone says so.

Each summer he tries to teach me to surf, or at least to master my boogie board, but nothing beats the rush I get from bodysurfing. Arms stretched out in front of me, head down, legs steering, whizzing through the waves. It's magic!

I remember one amazing day last summer when a pod of dolphins joined me on a wave.

It was the best thing ... we torpedoed through the water, and I could hear the dolphins squealing and clicking to each other. There were calves and mothers.

I've even done a couple of paintings of that day.

A splashing sound surprises me. I look across as Dave thunders past. He's at least five yards in front now. I shake my head. I've been dreaming. Again! I search for the buoy and realize I'm drifting into the rip. Again!

"Wake up," I tell myself. "FOCUS!!"

My legs give everything they have, and I manage to paddle across the dragging current before it sucks me in.

I slow for a moment to catch my breath. The others are way ahead. I'm last again.

I look back. The surf club flags are tiny. My legs feel like fishing line sinkers, trying to drag me down.

Finally, I reach the first buoy and begin paddling toward the second. Somehow I have to find the energy to finish.

I think about the dolphins. How they turn everything into a game. "This is *fun*," I tell myself. "You *want* to do it. You *chose* to do it!" I can't really convince myself, but muttering helps me make it to the second buoy.

I turn for shore, keeping an eye on the waves behind me, so I can try to ride them home.

Chapter Five

The Final Stretch

I reach the shallows, roll off the scratchy board into the water, and stumble up the beach.

As I drop my board, I look at the flag I'm meant to run to. My legs wobble and I realize that it's no use. I can't do it. I kneel in the sand and hang my head, trying not to cry. I'm so close to finishing, but I just can't make it!

I sniff back my tears, and for a moment all I can hear is my rushing pulse. Then someone begins clapping. Others join in. I look up. Everyone is clapping! For me.

Somehow I stand. Then I start slowly running, along that line of clapping people. I stare at the flag and know that somehow I will reach it.

"Focus," I whisper. Left foot, plod. Right foot, plod …

I trudge through the hot sand, feeling each grain pulling at the soles of my feet.

My arm brushes the yellow and red fabric of the flag. Now the final stretch to the finish line. All I have to do is get back. Back to the crowd. Back to Dad.

I squint into the sunlight and focus on Dad's face. This isn't exactly the glorious end I'd imagined. In my version I wasn't gasping like a beached tuna, but I feel a final surge of adrenalin rush through my blood. The thump-thumping of my heart echoes in my head.

Dad's face is closer. Nearly there. Nearly …

I cross the line, and before my legs collapse, Dad's arm catches me. I lean into him and let his body support me.

"Well done, Zack," he whispers. "That was a gutsy effort. I'm proud of you."

I look around. Everyone is clapping, even Carl and Nathan.

Then I hear Nathan snicker. "Yeah, about time!" Carl mutters. They stop giggling when they see the ferocious look on our coach's face.

"Is that what you call sportsmanship, young men?" I hear our coach bellow. "Because it certainly isn't what *I* call sportsmanship ..."

Poor Nathan and Carl! I *almost* feel sorry for them.

Chapter Six

Zack, the Dreamer

So I did it! Sometimes I still can't believe that I actually finished the race. It's amazing what you can do when you set your mind to it – if you want it badly enough. The surf club season is over now, so there are no more competitions until next year. For seven months I can go back to floating and drifting.

Maybe I am a dreamer, but it doesn't seem such a bad thing anymore. After all, if you don't have dreams, how can you achieve anything? And I have plenty of dreams!

I'm not sure if I'll enter the race again next year. Who knows, maybe I'll surprise everyone with another burst of determination.

Until then, I'll pull on my wetsuit and be happy doing what I like most. Floating about, watching what goes on under the waves, then drawing a bit, writing a bit, thinking a bit ...